Praying Together

Ideas for Developing Family Prayer in Your Home

Karla Hardersen

LTP
LITURGY
TRAINING
PUBLICATIONS

Nihil Obstat
Reverend Mr. Daniel G. Welter, JD
Chancellor
Archdiocese of Chicago
March 12, 2018

Imprimatur
Very Reverend Ronald A. Hicks
Vicar General
Archdiocese of Chicago
March 12, 2018

The *Nihil Obstat* and *Imprimatur* are declarations that the material is free from doctrinal or moral error, and thus is granted permission to publish in accordance with c. 827. No legal responsibility is assumed by the grant of this permission. No implication is contained herein that those who have granted the *Nihil Obstat* and *Imprimatur* agree with the content, opinions, or statements expressed.

This book was edited by Margaret M. Brennan. Michael A. Dodd was the production editor, and Kari Nicholls was the designer and production artist.

Cover illustration by Kari Nicholls based on art by Grace Wischmeyer (p. 6). Interior photographs by Karla Hardersen and drawings by Grace Wischmeyer.

22 21 20 19 18   1 2 3 4 5

Printed in the United States of America

Library of Congress Control Number: 2018944906

ISBN 978-1-61671-428-4

PRT

Contents

Introduction

When writing this book, one song came back to me over and over again. My children sang it in their atrium classes with Catechesis of the Good Shepherd when they were very young, and we sang it at home on repeat. The song goes to the tune of "This Fine Day."

> *Thank you God for giving us* _____,
> *Thank you God for giving us* _____,
> *Thank you God for giving us* _____,
> *Right where we are.*
>
> *Alleluia Praise the Lord,*
> *Alleluia Praise the Lord,*
> *Alleluia Praise the Lord,*
> *Right where we are.*

In their catechesis sessions, the blanks in the song were filled with the names of the children present. One by one, the verse went through using a child's name, and we thanked God for their presence in our little community. We continued singing and using hand motions, using the next child's name, going around our little circle of faith until we thanked God for each child. Each week, the children's faces lit up in great joy as we sang their name, and they lit up with equal joy as each of their friends' names were sung. It was a moment of presence in each other, part of our prayer time each week, a time of joy.

Every week, my children would get in the car after their time had ended and sing that song on repeat all the way home, using the names of their family members, their friends at school, everyone they knew. When they ran out of names, they started in on other things they were thankful for, first on a grander scale—the sky, the earth, the flowers, the rain, the sun—and then in a more proximate way—for their books, their school, the library, their lunch, etc.

Some days I sang along with them and encouraged them to think of people or things that they were thankful for that needed more direction—perhaps the crossing guard at school, or the neighbor that we often waved at but seldom talked to. Or for the clothes that we had and the shoes we put on our feet every day. And some days, they were creative enough to have an endless source of things they were thankful for. Some days, I believed the song would never end.

When our young children learn something at school, in art, on a sports team, or in music class, they learn faster and their skills improve quickly, becoming more innate and more natural when they repeat, use, or practice their newfound knowledge or skills outside of the classroom. In the same way, prayer is a part of our spiritual life that can be fostered, encouraged, and practiced outside of our more "structured" moments like Sunday Mass or weekly catechesis. Prayer is embedded in our rituals of faith in the Liturgy of the Word, in the Eucharist, in the Lord's Prayer that we pray together as a church community, in the songs that we sing at Mass, and in the moments that we hold hands, bow our heads, and lift our hearts to the presence of God. But how do we foster this prayer in our homes and with our children?

It is my hope that this book might encourage parents to move Sunday's prayers into everyday lives, to commit themselves and their families to finding more opportunities for reflection and prayer, so that parents and children might all grow in faith, joy, wonder, and sureness of God's immediate presence in their lives together.

Praying with Your Family

In the family, faith accompanies every age of life, beginning with childhood: children learn to trust in the love of their parents. That is why it is so important that within their families parents encourage shared expressions of faith which can help children gradually to mature in their own faith. Young people in particular, who are going through a period in their lives which is so complex, rich and important for their faith, ought to feel the constant closeness and support of their families and the Church in their journeys of faith.

—Pope Francis, *The Light of Faith*, no. 53

Parents desirous of nurturing the faith of their children are sensitive to their patterns of growth, for they know that spiritual experience is not imposed but freely proposed. It is essential that children actually see that, for their parents, prayer is something truly important. Hence moments of family prayer and acts of devotion can be more powerful for evangelization than any catechism class or sermon.

—Pope Francis, *The Joy of Love*, no. 288

Rejoice always, pray without ceasing, give thanks in all circumstances; for this is the will of God in Christ Jesus for you.

—1 Thessalonians 5:16–18

*P*rayer is at the heart of spiritual experience. It is experienced liturgically in Mass on Sundays when we listen to the Word as a community, when we hold hands, bow our heads, open our hearts, and speak the words that Jesus taught us, and when we break bread at the table of the Lord. As a Catholic community, we share these experiences with each other weekly, with those seated near us and those around the globe who share in the same universal rites.

Many of us pray regularly, quietly, in the stillness of our hearts, beyond the prayers of Sunday Mass. We speak to God using words we were taught from catechesis, or perhaps with our own voices. We find comfort, solace, peace, and hope in prayer. Prayer is our moment of resting in God's presence. It is our attempt to seek a relationship with and talk with God. It is a crucial aspect of our spiritual existence. It is essential in our homes and in our day-to-day life.

Prayer binds us in relationship with God. As we learn to pray, to speak with God more freely, more honestly and openly, we grow stronger in faith, trust, reverence, gratitude, and love of God. Prayer opens communication between us and God, joining us as if with a piece of thread. Every moment that we pray with our hearts, the thread connecting us strengthens.

Encouraging our own children into a prayer life is like weaving a new thread, tying them to God. As with our own prayer life, our children's strengthens as we practice and develop in prayer. This invisible thread does not simply exist between the child and God—but between parent and child, growing, strengthening, weaving a connection between their lives. At Sunday Mass, threads are created amongst the families as we gather and pray as a community, binding us to each other and to God. As our communal prayers look outside of our community, strands of thread are thrown outside our proximate relationships, towards our neighbors and others that we lift up. As we expand our prayers, as we strengthen and sustain our threads that we have weaved through our prayers, our lives become beautifully entwined in a tapestry of relationship, faith, and love.

Prayer is an intrinsic part of the Christian life. Talking to God is an acknowledgment of God's presence in our daily lives. Communicating our thoughts, needs, struggles, and desires is an affirmation of God's central role in our very being. Prayer strengthens the bonds between parents and children, families and God, families and the Church, and is therefore very much rooted in relationship. Developing any relationship takes effort and dedication. Teaching children to develop a relationship with God—to pray without ceasing— takes an even greater commitment, particularly as it requires our own dedication. Essential to understanding how parents and children can develop a family prayer life together, hand in hand, is understanding the relational bonds that are formed and nurtured through prayer. Therefore, understanding the most basic relational aspects of prayer is paramount to understanding prayer's importance in the Catholic life.

CHILD AND PARENT Children first learn how to pray through their most proximate relationship—their parents. Whether it is a prayer before each meal, a prayer for a loved one during the day, a song of praise sung while moving around the house, or a prayer before bed, children first identify the importance of communicating with God through their relationship with their parents. Parents truly are their children's first catechists and domestic theologians, a role both empowering and daunting. But more important than the theological dogma (and perhaps even the actual prayer that was offered), prayer spoken between parent and child brings families closer to each other in faith, trust, and love of God. Prayer strengthens familial bonds, tying each member to each other in a concrete, absolute way. To share and open one's hearts with each other in prayer affirms a deeply rooted love and commitment to the familial relationship.

CHILD AND GOD God is always present in all persons, and to openly communicate with God through prayer is to recognize that God is acting in all situations, and that we are to respond accordingly. Instilling in children an awareness that God is present in a tangible way in all situations, times, and places, and that we are to respond to that presence in both prayer and our actions, is to forge an understanding intrinsic in the child that God is ever present and with them always. Recognizing God as a sure source of love and trust in every moment is the gift of prayer to a child. A child knows, through prayer, that he or she is not alone and that God is a genuine presence in their lives. Love and trust grow as the relationship through prayer is fostered and encouraged.

FAMILIES AND THE CHURCH As individual families grow in their relationships with each other and with God, they are invited each week into a relationship with their larger Church community at Mass. Families of all shapes and sizes join together in prayer with their larger community. Liturgical and community prayers join every member of the congregation together as one body in Christ. Families together create a community of catechists, all entrusted with bringing new life into the Church.

THE CHURCH AND THE WORLD Each individual church is joined by a world-wide communion of churches, all participating in the same communal rites and prayers together. This universal, global Catholic Church is a network of communities of God that are unified through a common voice— our shared prayer.

THE WORLD AND THE CHILD This relational aspect of prayer starts out small and intimate, and branches out into a network of families, communities, churches, and global participation. It is important to recognize the child in relation to the world. The child, through prayer, is connected to God and to all members of the global Catholic community on the same faith journey. What begins as a tangible, intimate relationship grows into the acknowledgement that each child is part of a universal people of faith and therefore is both one *of many* and one *with many*. Each child has a distinct and defined role in the great community of faith. Each child's unique contributions are necessary for the whole of the Church to be a movement of God's presence, love, and faith in the world.

Prayer is relational. It is the thread that binds us to each other—both proximate and global—and to God. That children are both participants and creators in that relationship is vital to understanding the importance of encouraging and embracing a fulfilling prayer life in the home. Without prayer—without the voices of children adding to the chorus—our connectedness to each other, to our community, and to God, withers and greys. Children inject a vibrancy and vitality to our faith that we must nurture with utmost care and urgency.

Developing a Family Prayer Life

Parents are, "by word and example, to be the first preachers of the faith that their children hear" (*Lumen Gentium*, no. 11). Families are the "little churches," the domestic church, where parents act as minister, catechist, theologian, tasked with the spiritual upbringing of their children. Parents are the primary weavers, guiding the child with the necessary instructions in how to forge these threads, these relationships.

Children first learn how to pray, and learn the importance of prayer, from their parents. The latter may be achieved through simply and visibly practicing it in the home and making it a daily priority. But how do you pray? How do parents help build a family prayer life, nurturing and gently encouraging their children to individually participate in their own relationship with God? And how do parents do this when they struggle to do the same in their own lives? Where do parents begin?

Such an enormously important task can be an overwhelming weight on many parents. Parents might realize the importance of prayer, but that knowledge itself is an obstacle when feeling inadequately equipped to be their child's primary theologian. Compounding this, much of the available material for a family-based devotional life assumes an understanding of the domestic church that is ideal—i.e., that there are two parents, equally committed and firm in their beliefs, of the same faith, with a comprehensive understanding of theology, who have ample time to devote to praying with their family.

In reality, families are not so ideal and absolute. Many families today differ drastically from the idea of a nuclear family. Rather than a two-parent household, many families are led by single parents, or extended family members. And, as interfaith families are more prevalent than ever, religious differences make it difficult for many to initiate a shared, comprehensive direction of prayer life. Even in families where religious background is similar, a sureness of faith and theology cannot be assumed, which compounds parental differences and limitations. Practicing prayer at home with children today can be quite different than the more rigid catechism that many parents were taught. Bridging the gap between their own childhood understanding of prayer and their parental desire to acknowledge the individual needs of their own children is a difficult task. Pope Francis acknowledged this in *The Joy of Love*, writing, "Education in the faith has to adapt to each child, since older resources and recipes do not always work" (no. 288).

Perhaps the largest obstacle to families wishing to develop a family prayer life is simply a lack of time. Life today is so full of busyness—jobs, school, sports, after-school activities, carpools, homework—that sitting down for a thorough, well-prepared prayer service, using traditionally complex at-home prayers and rites is just unrealistic and impractical.

> Raising children calls for an orderly process of handing on the faith. This is made difficult by current lifestyles, work schedules, and the complexity of today's world where many people keep a frenetic pace just to survive. Even so, the home must continue to be the place where we learn to appreciate the meaning and beauty of the faith to pray and to serve our neighbor.
>
> —Pope Francis, *The Joy of Love*, no. 287

But is it possible for families to still have an active prayer life? Can we commit ourselves to a regular, daily prayer life and help our children develop a connection to God through prayer? That there is a desire among parents and families today is of no doubt. Can a domestic prayer life exist in a way that nurtures and speaks to the families and reality in which we live? To all these questions, I would offer a resounding yes! It is my hope that this book might offer guidance to all those families and parents asking these questions, that they may move forward in their prayer life together.

Forms of Prayer

Praying Together: Ideas for Developing Family Prayer in Your Home focuses on how a parent might develop a prayer life with their child. We will start by identifying common components or aspects of prayer. As I hope will be made clear throughout this book, there is no right or wrong way to pray. Prayer is simply talking to God, resting in God's presence. Communicating with God is a relationship that must be fostered and encouraged in any way—to limit it or attempt to restrict it to rigid parameters is to limit the growth and faith one has in God. Prayer is good, always. For those that struggle to pray— and those who struggle to teach their children to pray—the following forms of prayer may help give a more cohesive shape to the prayer, a means of focusing prayer. They are by no means meant to restrict.

According to the *Catechism of the Catholic Church* (nos. 2623– 2649), there are five types of Christian prayer:

BLESSINGS Because God blesses us, we can in turn bless God, our Creator. We adore God because God is great, and we are dependent on God in all things. Prayers of blessings are prayers of worship. Our liturgy during the Mass is full of worship, most easily heard in the Gloria when we sing, "Glory to God in the Highest!"

Prayers of blessings include expressions of faith and trust in God. The Apostles' Creed begins with such an expression: "We believe in God . . ." The Bible is rich with prayers of blessings:

> Blessed be the Lord, the God of Israel,
> Who alone does wondrous things,
> Blessed be his glorious name forever;
> May his glory fill the whole earth.
> Amen and Amen.
>
> —Psalm 72:18–19

PRAISE Similar to blessings, prayers of praise recognize that our love for God goes beyond what God does. We love and praise God simply because God IS. Most of the Psalms that we read and sing during the liturgy are prayers of praise:

I will extol you, my God and King,
And bless your name forever and ever.
Every day I will bless you,
And praise your name forever and ever.
Great is the Lord, and greatly to be praised.

—Psalm 145:1–3

I will bless the Lord at all times;
His praise shall continually be in my mouth.

—Psalm 34:1

From the rising of the sun to its setting
The name if the Lord is to be praised.

—Psalm 113:3

PETITION Prayers of petition (or requests, appeals) are prayers that most people are familiar with. Petitions are not necessarily about asking God for spiritual or personal needs, but are more about recognizing God's presence in acknowledging that we receive all from God.

Do not worry about anything, but in everything by prayer and supplication with thanksgiving, let your requests be made known to God.

—Philippians 4:6

Prayer of petitions acknowledge that we must turn to God in all things—not to get what we want, but, as Jesus taught, for "thy will be done." The *Catechism* mentions three movements of prayers of petition: First, that we ask forgiveness. In confessing our wrongs, our humility brings us into right relation to God and with each other. Second, that our prayers identify with the movement of the Christian to search for the Kingdom of God. All that we petition, all that we ask is in service of bringing about the reign of God—"Thy Kingdom come, Thy will be done." And third, all true needs can be petitioned to God, and we are counseled to therefore pray at all times.

INTERCESSIONS Intercessions are prayers on behalf of others. They are an expression of Christian fellowship and recognize God's loving mercy. During the liturgy, the Prayer of the Faithful raises prayers of intercession as an expression of the prayers of the entire community. These prayers recognize the requests to God for the Church, the world, and those in need. The congregation affirms those prayers together, as one united heart.

THANKSGIVING Prayers of Thanksgiving invoke a spirit of gratitude, of thankfulness for God's many blessings. These prayers are scattered throughout the liturgy and are common in the home as well, particularly before a meal. Every moment of one's life can become a moment of thanksgiving, and thereby of prayer.

> I will give thanks to the Lord with my whole heart;
> I will tell of all your wonderful deeds.
> I will be glad and exult in you;
> I will sing praise to your name, O Most High.
> —Psalm 9:1–2

> Let us come into his presence with thanksgiving;
> Let us make a joyful noise to him with songs
>   of praise!
> —Psalm 95:2

> O give thanks to the Lord, for he is good;
> For his steadfast love endures forever.
> —1 Chronicles 16:34

These normative forms of prayer from the *Catechism* can help give families a broad understanding of how prayer in the Christian life can be expressed, as evidenced through Scripture. All of them are present in our Catholic liturgical and spiritual traditions, but they are also meant to be enacted at home. A family prayer might include one of these categories, it might combine several, or it may be difficult to place in any category. These prayer types offer us a basic starting point of understanding from which we might go forward and begin to develop our own understanding of prayer as it might exist in the home.

Sowing the Seeds at Home

Without prayer, you cannot be connected or you cannot remain united with the Lord. It's absolutely essential.

—Joseph Cardinal Bernadin, *The Gift of Peace*

Essential to a domestic prayer life is that it must be one that encourages all members—both adults and children, to grow in faith and prayer together. It cannot assume any individual is the designated leader (or most knowledgeable), but must enable all members to learn and develop individually and collectively in relation to God, with each other, with the Church, and with the world. Fostering an understanding of prayer as communication and relationship with God—as threads connecting one to another—would help each family to learn, listen, and spend time in God's presence in their own way, time, and place.

To help children develop these threads, while at the same time developing our own relationship with God, takes work. But it is the work that results in the dearest, most loving union with God that will be the cornerstone of a child's faith, and a pillar of steadfastness throughout their life. Talking to God should be easy. It should be as instinctive as breathing—but it takes time and dedication to develop.

Where to begin on this prayer journey? How do we take our knowledge of prayer through the Mass on Sunday, from the Bible, or from our catechesis and transform it in a way that makes it palpable and simple enough for a child to fully participate in at home? And even more than to simply participate, for the child to be the advocate for his or her own faith journey—to be young theologians, discovering the joy, wonder, and wisdom of God in their own time?

The following chapters will attempt a comprehensive approach to such a prayer journey for any family. It will offer parents and families insights into how they might make prayer a more intrinsic part of their daily life, developing the understanding of prayer as communication and relationship with God, thereby growing in faith and relation to God and with each other.

Faith has the power to both define and inform who we are. Drawing closer to God through prayer more fully recognizes God as our Creator, Redeemer, and Sustainer. God as the One whom we move towards. As Catholics, it is our most central relationship. We must nurture it. We must teach our children how to seek that relationship—how to cultivate it—and we must walk the journey with them.

# Finding Grace in the Ordinary

When my oldest daughter was younger, we would frequently go out to the yard and work on the garden together while her younger siblings were down for their morning naps. One particular day, my daughter asked, "Mama, where is God?" I remember putting down my gardening gloves and shovel, taking her hand, sitting her down on the porch, sitting next to her, and asking her where she thought God was. She looked out across the yard, her tiny forehead creased in concentration, and thought for a few moments. Then she said, very matter of factly, "I think God must be in the rain. It makes everything grow!" I remember being awestruck by her words. Such clarity and sureness in her voice, and such a complex theological question brought to simplicity by a four-year-old. I quickly agreed with her and asked her where else might God be? She looked around and said, "In the flowers!" I asked her why, and she responded, "Because they're so beautiful!"

I encouraged her to tell me more places where God was, and she quickly filled my ears with so many responses—in the trees, in the sunshine, in the butterflies, in the sky, and in the robin that was looking for a worm for its chicks. With each response, she would have an explanation as to why God was there—because God grows so big, because God is so full of light, because God was in the small things, because God was everywhere, and because God takes care of us and gives us food. I asked her where all of these things came from and she said, "God made everything, even me!" I then asked her what we should do when we were given such gifts. She said quickly, "Say thank you!" She quickly grabbed my hand and prayed, "Thank you God for all these amazing things! Amen!" And then she jumped up and went right back to work in the garden.

This interaction with my daughter encouraged me to not only be more intentional and creative with our conversation about God, but to listen to what my daughter has to say about God. Her theology was simple. She saw God in the things around her because she had some preconceived understandings of who God was—big, light, small, all encompassing, nurturing, creator. She reminded me of the simplicity of faith, to open my eyes more to the wonders of God's creation, and that God is not only Creator, but also present in creation.

Nurturing a child's prayerful heart starts with simplicity —talking about God, seeking God in the everyday, responding to God by creating moments of prayer, and embracing a child's imagination and creativity on their prayer journey. Parents, with their children following their lead, must engage in intentional God moments. Parents must encourage their children on their prayer journey.

Seeking God in the Everyday

A place to begin growing a family prayer life is to make God visible and present in daily life so that children recognize and see God in the world. This is an important aspect to faith that I think sometimes we as adults forget: God has created all things, and is in all things; "the whole earth is full of his glory" (Isaiah 6:3). Helping children to see God everywhere is to introduce them to a God that is ever present and always nearby. It is a way of first building a relationship by seeing God as someone in their everyday lives, not someone that is just at church on Sundays. As we begin to introduce our children to God, who is always near, we as adults are reminded that God is always nearby as well, deepening and recommitting ourselves in relation to God.

God is a presence that is always acting, always present, always working in the world. Where do we see God? How is God working in the world? An important distinction must be made here. We want to encourage our children to find God, to see God in all things. We do not want our children to develop an understanding of God as a Santa Claus–like figure who is always watching and judging us based on our behavior. That is an unhealthy image that I believe many children and adults have grown up envisioning. God is always present, always moving in the world, and God can see all things. But to entertain a theology of God as a constant judge and punisher is psychologically and spiritually destructive.

To help our children find grace in the ordinary, to find God present and at work in our daily lives, takes time and commitment on behalf of the parent. It is not meant to be something reserved just for Sundays. Yes, God is present when a community of believers is gathered in God's name, and such moments are incredibly important and instrumental for the faith development of any child. But seeking God *at work in the everyday* is particularly vital to a child's prayer life. It initiates the understanding that God is everywhere, in all things, and we, as Catholic Christian followers, are to respond to that presence accordingly.

The knowledge to a child that God is with them, in all places and things, is the beginnings of the relationship that we foster and develop through prayer. There are many ways in which a parent might introduce their child to the presence of God. The following are suggestions and methods that I have found to be helpful in my family's own journey of faith. What I believe is important to understand is that the child has an imagination, creativity, and a genuine understanding of God that I would argue surpasses that of many an adult. A parent's gift to the child is to walk along beside them, encouraging and leading, but also listening, learning, and seeing the wonders and joy of God through their child.

Prayer Walk

Much like my daughter did in the garden, a prayer walk involves finding God in our surroundings and understanding that God is both Creator and in all of creation. It helps the child obtain an understanding of God that they can relate to, and it helps them identify qualities of God that they can understand. Prayer walks can begin at a very early age and are an ideal way in helping bring God to the forefront of a child's everyday life. If we can begin both the conversation and our relationship with God by recognizing that God is near us always, it prepares the child for a lifetime of knowing that God is always with us.

There are many ways to implement a prayer walk, but at its simplest, it's a walk talking about God's creations. It can take place in the backyard, in the neighborhood, through a nature trail, or down a city street. A parent might ask a child similar questions:

- Where do you see God?

- Where do you think God is?

- How is God like this particular item?

- Why do you think God might have created this item?

- How does this item make you feel?

Children might have an easy time selecting various items, but if not, a parent can guide them.

Frequently, with my own children, we started with smaller items, like a worm, rock, or flower, and moved to larger, grander ideas, like trees, the sky, the sun. Children have so much to say if we gently prod them and ask simple questions.

Children have rich imaginations, and a prayer walk is a way to channel their creativity into their faith life. Not only will a prayer walk foster their relationship with God, but it will also encourage them to imagine God and capture the wonder, joy, and love of God's creation. As parents, we have a unique opportunity through our children to once again see God's glory through the eyes of a child, through their awe, excitement, curiosity, and amazement. These prayer walks connect both parent and child to God's creation and give an opportunity not only to discuss God, but to thank God for all God has made.

A Prayerful Response

Once a child is able to see and realize God's proximity in their physical lives, we can move toward one of our responses to God—prayer. My daughter's simple prayer, "Thank you God for all these amazing things! Amen!" is one such response. Instilling a simple cause-and-effect reaction—we see that God is present, therefore, we respond—is an important communicative tool in our relational development with God. I think as adults we sometimes have a hard time with this—we go through our incredibly busy lives so quickly and are exhausted by day's end that we seldom have time to respond to God at work in our life. But if we could take the time to instill this in our children (and consequently work on acknowledging the relational aspect in our own lives), they will have a greater chance of responding to God more fully as they grow. Helping our children in both *seeing* God in the world, and *responding*, is one of the greatest spiritual gifts we can give them.

Often, these prayer responses are spontaneous. Children have the simplest and most meaningful of prayers, if only we can encourage them to speak them freely. Some children might be timid or not know what to say. As parents, we can encourage them with the hope that with time and frequency, they will be able to say them on their own. Prayers of thanksgiving or praise are particularly appropriate here. Though these prayer walks begin with the parent, the hope is that children will continue these on their own, gaining a sense of awareness of God's presence throughout their lives, learning to respond to God with prayer.

Everyday Moments of Prayer

By seeking God in the everyday moments of life, the intention is to bring about God as a normative presence and relationship that is relevant throughout our day. We need to talk about God frequently and with intention if our family is to have an enriched and abiding prayer life.

There are many moments that we experience daily that we can use as additional opportunities to pray with our children. The hope is that by responding with prayer to a particular occasion, our children might develop conversation with God as a reflex, a habit. Of course, it is intimidating to begin this with our children when we ourselves might not have been as committed in our own prayer life, or are unsure of even how to pray. But to have a full prayer life, one does not need to understand systematic theology or have a thorough understanding of the Bible. Praying is about opening oneself to communication with God—being willing to talk to God, to be in relationship with God. Fancy words are not needed. What you bring to the prayer is *enough as you are*, always. Whether you have a sureness of faith or you feel inadequate, this is a journey that you can take with your child. It requires only willingness and faith to pray with your children. The rest you and your family will learn together as you go.

Every moment is an opportunity to pray. This is not to say that we are to force our children to pray at every moment. Praying should be a natural process of conversation with God, when opportunities arise. One such moment that I grew up learning was when we heard the sound of a firetruck, ambulance, or police siren, we would pray for all those involved. It became a conditioned response in me, that when I hear a siren, I pray immediately. My children have learned this from me as well, and I hope it has become an instinctual prayer moment for them.

There are an infinite number of opportunities throughout the course of our days where we might reach out to our children to pray, helping them to recognize that God is always present. The following moments are times when we can guide our children to pray so they can develop a more intimate relation with God. Our busy lives make it impossible to pray at every single one of these moments, but I encourage you to attempt to pray with your children as frequently as possible. The more we are able to pray with them, the more they will understand that prayer is an important part of their lives. And they will hopefully begin to pray on their own.

MORNINGS/EVENINGS When we begin and end our day with prayer, we reinforce to our children the importance of God in our daily lives. When our children wake, we can pray to thank God for a new day, a new beginning, and ask God to be with us throughout our day. It helps a family to center the day—and their hearts—with God first thing in the morning.

Likewise, a prayer together as a family at the end of the day serves to recap the day and once again recenter the family's commitment to and relation with God. Though I will provide more details into what a family prayer might look like at the end of the day in later chapters, one way to really focus the family, particularly with younger children, is to ask them, "Where did you see God today?" or "When did you feel God's presence today?" If those do not prompt many answers, or if the children seem to struggle, I find it easiest to ask, "When did you feel the happiest today?" After the child answers, it can then lead to further discussions about how God feels when we are happy and how we can respond to God when we are feeling joyful. I think these are simple conversations that we can have with our children at the close of the day that really help to reiterate that God is always present, and we can respond.

MEALS The most common occasion for family prayer is before meals. Whether you can pray together for all three meals, or can only manage one, it is important to begin this prayer with your family. You can say a traditional rote prayer that you might already know—for example, one from a book or the Bible—or you can say what is on your heart at the moment. It is an important prayer of blessing and thanksgiving to teach your children.

The New Testament is full of Jesus saying prayers over meals. In the Gospel of Matthew, Jesus "blessed and broke the loaves" when feeding the five thousand (14:19), and "after giving thanks he broke them and gave them to the disciples" when feeding the four thousand (15:36). During the Last Supper, Jesus gave thanks and blessed the bread and cup before sharing it as his Body and Blood with his disciples. On the road to Emmaus, Jesus once again took some bread and gave thanks.

Sharing in a meal by first giving thanks and blessing our food—just as Jesus did—is to give thanks to God for providing for us, acknowledging that God is the source of everything we have. Prayer over a meal connects us to each other and to God. Helping our children recognize this connectivity through prayers of thanksgiving and blessing is an important daily reminder of God's presence in our lives.

SCHOOL OR OTHER ACTIVITY Before we part with our children before school, or after school activities, dance class, or soccer practice, it can be beneficial to pray with our children first. We can pray that we might feel God's presence with us as we journey throughout our day, and that our minds, eyes, ears, lips, and feet be vessels of God's goodness to everyone we meet. Children need encouragement to recognize that God is not just at home or at church, but in all areas of our lives, and that we are always to recognize and respond to God's presence. God is with us, in the activities we do, in the subjects that we learn, and in the people that we meet. Praising God for all of the goodness we experience, and being thankful for all that we receive, is a prayer that we can instill in our children at a very early age.

EMOTIONS It would do our children well if we could respond to our many emotions throughout the day with prayer. If our children are happy, joyful, or excited about something, we can say a quick prayer of blessing or thanksgiving—"Thank you

Jesus for our happy hearts!" These daily moments of prayer do not have to be complex or wordy. They can be a simple recognition that we see that God is the source of all that we do, and we are thankful for God's presence in our lives.

The times our children are sad or hurt are also moments when we can pray with them, letting them know that God is with them when they are in need. "When they call to me, I will answer them; I will be with them in trouble" (Psalm 91:15).

Many adults have a difficult time talking about their pain. How much more, then, are the difficulties in verbalizing compounded when it is a child? As parents, we can talk it through with them, we can listen, and we can be with our children as they struggle. But we can also pray with them. Holding their hands, asking God to be with them, helping them to verbalize their needs in prayer gives healing and comfort. It lets them know that they are not alone, that God is always with them, even in their sorrows.

Fear is another emotion that is particularly difficult for a child to experience. The Bible tells us to not be afraid, that God is with us:

> Be strong and courageous; do not be frightened or dismayed,
> for the Lord your God is with you wherever you go.
>
> —Joshua 1:9

> Do not fear, for I am with you, do not be afraid, for I am your
> God; I will strengthen you, I will help you.
>
> —Isaiah 41:10

> I sought the Lord and he answered me,
> And delivered me from all my fears.
>
> —Psalm 34:4

To a young child who is afraid of the dark, afraid of school, in an unfamiliar setting, or doing something alone for the first time, fear can be a disability. As parents, we can reassure them that God is always with them, that they do not have to be afraid. But these words can sometimes not be enough. Praying with them (as well as for them) when they are afraid can help alleviate their stress and calm their heart. It opens them to a comfort through God that we cannot necessarily provide on our own. Using prayer frequently in these situations can help condition their spirit and let them know that they are loved, and that God is with them.

Similarly, when children experience worry or anxiousness, prayer can be a powerful catalyst to calming and healing their hearts and spirits, bringing them the peace of God.

> Do not worry about anything, but in everything in prayer and supplication with thanksgiving let your requests be made known to God. And the peace of God, which surpasses all understanding, will guard your hearts and your minds in Christ Jesus.
>
> —Philippians 4:6–7

> Peace I leave with you; my peace I give to you. I do not give to you as the world gives. Do not let your hearts be troubled, and do not let them be afraid.
>
> —John 14:27

How do we bring them the peace of God? How do they feel it enough in their inner being so that they are no longer afraid? Prayer has the ability to connect the child to God, bringing peace and calm to a worried heart. Parents have the responsibility of recognizing the worry and the need to bring these difficulties to God in prayer. Children need to be prompted to pray when they are hurting, with the hope that in time, they will be able to pray one day on their own when they recognize that they are in need. It provides such comfort and security to a child, knowing that God is with them always.

> So do not worry about tomorrow, for tomorrow will bring worries of its own. Today's trouble is enough for today.
>
> —Matthew 6:34

SICK OR INJURED Prayer has healing power, particularly the healing that comes from knowing you are not alone. Jesus said, "Come to me, all you who are weary and burdened, and I will give you rest" (Matthew 11:28). When children are sick or have an injury, or when they are hurting, we can take that illness as another moment to pray with them. Again, the hope is that the child will recognize God's presence even in their illness and will turn to God for comfort, healing, and strength. We can help foster this sense of relationship by offering a simple prayer of healing with our children.

All of these moments—mornings and evenings, meals, school, activities, moments of emotions, and illness—are regular events in the life of a family. They happen frequently, if not daily, and are occasions in which families can introduce prayer as a part of a family's faith life. I believe that once children are exposed to praying outside of Mass, they will find many more places where they wish to pray. Parents, follow their lead! God can be and should be a normative presence in your household—and it is possible with a commitment to prayer.

Recognizing God as present in our everyday, simple lives encourages children to a relationship with God that is real, tangible, and intentional. Helping children to not only see God in all things around them, but to respond to God's presence

through prayer, is to lead them on a prayer journey that will both enrich and inform their lives.

The role of the parent in this particular part of the prayer life is primarily to lead through example. Children will not learn to pray—either in Church or in the home—if they do not witness it through their parents. I encourage parents to take the time and make the effort to be diligent in prayer during their child's formative years. In all the above moments of prayer, a parent is to journey with their children, walking alongside them in faith, encouraging them, sometimes asking questions and gently prodding for answers. There are no specific words that must be used. There is no right or wrong prayer, there is only the said and unsaid.

Children will learn quickly through witnessing and participating in the family's prayer life. The hope is that children will develop a concrete and sure relationship with God that will carry them into their adult years. Children should be able to recognize God's presence at work in the world in their daily life and respond to that presence through prayer.

Reflection Questions and Suggestions

Consider your surroundings. What is a possible location for a prayer walk? Your backyard, your neighborhood, a forest preserve, or a city block.

Take your own prayer walk to reflect on God's presence in your life.

Consider your family's daily schedule. Which everyday moments of prayer are possible?

Find moments for you and your children to talk with God through prayer throughout the day:

- ❀ **Where did you find God today?**
- ❀ **What gifts from God did you see today?**
- ❀ **What should we say to God for these gifts?**

What should we say to God during the following moments of our day?

- ❀ **Morning**
- ❀ **Evening**
- ❀ **Before or after meals**
- ❀ **Before or after school**
- ❀ **Other daily activities**

What other daily moments can your family use as a time to talk to God?

How can we talk with God when we are happy, sad, afraid, worried, or sick?

 Bringing Prayer into Your Home

Called to Be a Domestic Church

Nurturing a child's prayerful heart starts with simplicity—talking about God, finding God in the everyday, finding moments of prayer, and learning to respond to God's presence with prayer. Parents must engage in intentional God moments with their children. It is encouraged that the prayer moments in the previous chapter happen frequently, some even daily (such as prayer before meals), so that we and our children become comfortable recognizing and talking to God in our daily lives. In this chapter, we will explore what facilitates creating an environment for prayer in the home.

Our Catholic tradition offers us a beautiful moment each week when we, a community of faith, gather to pray together, not only as part of a single parish community, but as a universal Church across the globe. In our Sunday Masses we are called by name to the Table, our spirits are rejuvenated by the Gospel, we pray together as one voice, and we reaffirm our mission to go and *do* church in the world. The Mass is our Catholic faith's ultimate act of worship—and we participate in it as a community of believers.

And the family—the home—is intended to be a domestic church. Finding spontaneous moments of prayer throughout our day when we can both talk about God and talk with God is essential in developing our children's spirituality, faith, and relationship with God, however we must also find time to pray as a family community. A designated time and place for praying together as a family can shape the entire family's sense of being. We must also choose to put God in our family's life in a way that transforms and centers our family's purpose and identity.

Being a domestic church takes concentrated earnest effort. A family is, just as the Church, a community of believers and a community of love. The home is the foundation to the broader Church family. It is where the members—particularly the youngest ones—can raise their questions about God and their faith, where their beliefs can find root, and their doubts have a place to be voiced. The *Catechism* states:

> The Christian family constitutes a specific revelation and realization of ecclesial communion, and for this reason it can and should be called a domestic church. It is a community of faith, hope, and charity; it assumes singular importance in the Church, as is evident in the New Testament.
>
> —no. 2204

Parents as their children's first catechists and ministers are instrumental in instilling the importance of community and prayer in their lives. Families are encouraged to have a family prayer time from the beginning. Children are never too young to pray with their family (although their participation will vary based on age), and yet it is never too late to begin. Families must share the conviction that their faith is the framework for their identity as a familial unit, and be committed to bringing a sense of symmetry from their larger church community into their home.

Family Prayer Rituals

The domestic church—the "little church"—is the smallest body of the church, gathered to form a community of believers in Christ. The family does not simply *go* to Church, but the family is the church and is able to *do* church. The domestic church builds up the larger church by centering its members in faith and love of God. As Jesus states in the Gospel of Matthew, "For where two or three are gathered in my name, I am there among them" (18:20). Praying together as a family community places God at the ultimate center of the family's sense of worth and being.

The blessing of the domestic church is that it is able to focus on the children as equally important—if not centrally important—members of the community. I would suggest that the ultimate goal for children is that they wholly participate in the family prayer, and that they not simply be observers on the outside, as is frequently the case during Sunday Mass. They are active participants, even contributors and directors, of the prayer. Parents may be the catechists, but the children are the members who give the voice, life, and spirit into the family church. It is a blessing for the children when their voices are heard, and also a blessing for the parents and the larger Church community. We cannot minimize the importance of the child in the understanding of the Kingdom of God:

Then he took a little child and put it among them; and taking it in his arms, he said to them, "Whomever welcomes one such child in my name welcomes me, and whoever welcomes me welcomes not me but the one who sent me."

—Mark 9:36–37

"Let the little children come to me; do not stop them; for it is to such as these that the kingdom of God belongs. Truly I tell you, whoever does not receive the kingdom of God as a little child will never enter it."

—Mark 10:14–15

Family prayer, over all else, has the ability to transform the family's entire identity into a concentrated community of love and faith. Modern families are consumed by so many outside commitments. School, work, sports, band, plays, clubs, dance—there are endless activities and obligations for the parents and the children. At any moment, any of those activities has the potential to monopolize the time, energy, and life of the family. And while they may bring happiness to individual members (and even to several), they can seriously compromise the sense of shared commitment and communion among the members if they are considered to be what defines the family. Family prayer unifies each member and centralizes their entire communal sense of self as being one community of faith.

The Role of the Parent in Family Prayer

Education in the faith by the parents should begin in the
child's earliest years. This already happens when family members
help one another to grow in faith by the witness of a Christian
life in keeping with the Gospel. Family catechesis precedes,
accompanies, and enriches other forms of instruction in the
faith. Parents have the mission of teaching their children to
pray and to discover their vocation as children of God.

—*Catechism*, no. 2226

Parents are the first and primary catechists, ministers, and
theologians in their children's lives. Some parents may feel
ill-equipped to handle such responsibilities, but family prayer
can be simple enough for those of any theological background.
What is important is that parents *begin*—to the best of their
ability—to participate with their children in prayer. Without
the call to prayer by the parents in the home, children may
believe that prayer and a relationship with God are limited
to Sundays.

In creating a family prayer time, the parents need to attend
to the following:

TIME AND PLACE Parents must find time for their family to
spend together in prayer. I would offer that most families
would find just before bedtime to be ideal, but each must take
into account their own family needs and schedules. Whether
it be before bed, in the morning, or before or after a family
meal, it should be an intentional time reserved for prayer. To
instill a sense of regularity and ritual, it is best if the time is
consistent day to day (though of course, life happens and
schedules must be fluid). The length of the prayer itself needs
consideration. With the youngest children, only a few minutes

are needed for prayer. As the children age and become more involved, prayer may get lengthy. It is important for prayer to not feel rushed.

- *A Place for Prayer:* Family prayer time also needs to be held somewhere free from loud noises or visual distractions. Perhaps a corner of a living room might be designated for prayer, or even a bedroom. Wherever it is, ensure that the children are comfortable and that a peaceful, calm atmosphere can be maintained. Prayer can happen at any time and any place—but for the purpose of developing a daily time of family prayer, parents can attempt to plan this out in advance in order to optimize the conditions for centering children into a worship setting.

- *Setting the Tone:* It is normal that by the end of the day, the children are cranky and the adults exhausted. The house might be a mess, and there might be a list of things that still need to be accomplished. Parenting is messy and difficult. But in order for each member to be open to listening and talking to God, an attempt should be made to ensure that some sense of calm and peace can flow over each person. This can be achieved through dimming the lights and lighting candles, or simply by using a dedicated place for prayer. Quiet music or dimming the lights can be a cue for the children to settle. Finding what works for each family and using the same steps daily can help the children to focus on prayer.

- *Organizing the Prayer:* In order to ensure that this prayer circle is intentional and assist the children in knowing what to expect, parents should try to somewhat organize their family's prayer time. In the subsequent chapters,

I will detail a structure of family prayer that I find most helpful, but each family is unique, and I would encourage families to find what most creates for them a sense of community and God's presence. Again, life is sometimes less organized and more chaotic, so variances in prayer time and content are to be expected. I encourage each family to plan for the ideal situation and improvise as needed.

- *Preparation of Materials:* Depending on the needs of your individual family, parents might want to consider what will help define the prayer space and time. These can be candles, music, flowers for the prayer space, Bible passages or stories, songs, etc. In the end, all that is needed are the family members. But depending on the ages and needs of the children, the environment can help facilitate a prayerful tone.

- *Preparation of Content:* It is also useful to spend some moments thinking about what might be most beneficial to include in your prayer time. Perhaps a Bible reading from Mass on the previous Sunday or a passage from the upcoming Mass so the children might recognize it during the service. My children particularly loved to sing the songs from our Mass, so we would have the lyrics available when needed. If your child had a rough day, or is going through a difficult time, it might be helpful to find songs or passages that they might relate to during the prayer. Though this might seem like too much work to do on a daily basis, again—family prayer time can be rich and meaningful without any additional materials or content. But every once in a while, sparing a few minutes to prepare songs or readings that tie into their day or the Sunday Mass will help enrich their understanding of Church and how relevant God is in their lives.

- *Prayer Leader:* It is the parent's role to lead the children in prayer when the children are very young. With time and repetition, soon the children will enthusiastically plan and organize family prayer time almost entirely on their own—and that is what you want! Taking ownership of their own spiritual lives is an important step for every child. They might like to sing the same songs, or read the same prayers, or change things every day. As parents, you must lay the framework of prayer, introduce it, repeat it, and then when they are ready, encourage them to take on a larger role.

The Framework for Family Prayer

So far, we have looked at developing an understanding of prayer as relational, discussed engaging in intentional moments through finding grace in the ordinary and responding with prayer, and begun to outline the necessity of formalizing a structured, daily ritual of family prayer, fully embodying the notion of family as the domestic church. In the next several chapters, I will further outline a basic structure of a family prayer. This more ritualistic form of prayer will draw on key elements that I believe are instrumental in providing children with a rich, spiritual prayer life that ties into their need for a relationship with God and with a faith-based community.

From my experiences as a mother and as a catechist in the Catechesis of the Good Shepherd, I believe the following elements are ideal in creating a prayer life for both child and parent, and will encourage a sense of relation with God, community of faith, and spiritual fortitude of the family. They can be done in any order, though I recommend the order in which they are listed:

- *Peaceful Silence:* creating and sharing a moment of silence in prayer

- *Prayers of Gratitude:* thanking God for all God's goodness and presence in our lives

- *Intercessions:* praying on behalf of others

- *Reflection and Conversation:* a time to reflect, discuss, and ask questions about faith

- *Other Resources:* using other sources of spiritual insight

Each of these helps facilitate a reverent, prayerful space in which parents can be both model and participant. Children first learn about God by watching and imitating the immediate adults in their lives. This is a time—more intimate than the larger Sunday community—when the parents demonstrate their faith. It is time in which parents may witness their child's love and joy for God, and come to understand more fully the simplicity and wonder of faith.

The aim of this entire book is simple: to lead children and parents to pray together, so that both might fall in love with God and devote themselves more fully to living in right relation with God. A daily family prayer aims at deepening the relationship with the Good Shepherd and embodies the family as the domestic church. Children and parents are invited, through this prayer, to listen and respond to God's presence in their lives.

Reflection Questions and Suggestions

Be intentional to family prayer by reserving the time on your family calendar/planner.

Consider the locations available for your family prayer time. Which locations best offer a quiet and distraction-free area to set the tone for your family prayer time?

How is your family participating as a domestic church?

What from Sunday Mass can you include in your home?

What songs, readings, or items from your church (flowers, statues, linens, etc.) do your children respond to?

Creating a Peaceful Silence

Then the Lord said: Go out and stand on the mountain before the Lord; the Lord will pass by. There was a strong and violent wind rending the mountains and crushing rocks before the Lord—but the Lord was not in the wind; after the wind, an earthquake—but the Lord was not in the earthquake; after the earthquake, fire—but the Lord was not in the fire; after the fire, a light silent sound.

—1 Kings 19:11–12

Nearly every minute of every day in a family is filled with sound. Usually, they register in the "loud" category: talking, yelling, crying, laughing, singing, feet pounding, whistles blowing, phones ringing, television, coaches shouting, fans cheering, dishes clattering, dogs barking. Life is an endless stream of sound that desensitizes one to quiet. In the flurry of activities and the frenetic pace in which most families today operate, quiet does not happen easily. The Lord is in a "light silent sound"—akin to a whisper. How do we find this quiet in our loudness?

In the Psalms God tell us to be *still*. "Be still, and know that I am God" (46:10). Quiet and stillness—two very difficult things for children *and* adults. When my children were younger, the family that regularly sat in front of us at Sunday Mass had very lively, rambunctious kids who were constantly "whispering" far above even a very generous definition of the word, and who bounced around from family member to family member. One week, during the Sign of Peace, their visiting grandparent asked me, "How do you keep your kids so still and quiet? It's like these kids don't know how to quit!" Another week after the liturgy, a man came up to me laughing and told me he had enjoyed watching my children immensely during the service. Unbeknownst to me, two of my children had been fighting about holding hands during the Lord's Prayer. One wanted to hold the other's hand and the other wasn't having any part of it, one pulling and one yanking away. Evidently, one of my children eventually kicked the other one, who then finally agreed to hold hands. I was slightly mortified, and I have no idea how I missed witnessing that. I can only hope I was finding my own stillness and quiet in prayer, as my children certainly were not.

Often in the Catechesis of the Good Shepherd, we would use silence as a way to center our hearts and bodies before listening to the Word of God. We also used silence and calm, quiet bodies as the way to begin the time of communal prayer with the children. This silencing allowed all of us to listen for the voice of the Good Shepherd and put our hearts in a contemplative, prayerful place.

Many children—and, indeed, many adults—have a difficult time being still and quiet. How could they not? With a full day and movement and noise behind them, the brain and the body have a hard time shutting down. But the time of family prayer should begin with the quieting of mind and body in order to fully participate in prayer. That is not to say that God is not in the loudness and the busyness. Truly God is present in all situations; silence allows us to listen to God. Stillness in prayer is not forcing people to withhold sound, or forcing them to not move, nor is it the absence of all sound (in fact, quiet contemplative music may encourage the silence of the mind that prayer requires). Rather, to become silent or still acknowledges that prayer is both *talking* and *listening*—it is a conversation between all participants, including, and most especially, God. Prayer is a practice in learning stillness and quiet of mind, body, and spirit, of disengaging with the busyness of life and engaging in a real relationship with God.

Encouraging children to begin prayer in silence must come with the realization that it will take time to adjust to being still. At first they might only be able to maintain a peaceful silence for a minute, maybe even less. And that is okay. As your family does this regularly, it will become easier. Developing a prayerful silence can happen throughout the day—for example, immediately upon waking up, just before meals, or at moments when the stresses of life seem too much to endure are times to take a moment to recenter yourself. Encourage your children to do the same when they are struggling. The more frequent the practice, the more open you will become to God's presence.

Encouraging Quiet and Stillness with Children

Disengaging from the busyness of one's day and refocusing on the presence of Jesus takes effort, particularly with children. It is not that we want to teach them to be quiet or to be still for the sake of not hearing noise or for the sake no movement. It is to allow one's mind, body, and spirit to open itself to communication with Jesus and to become comfortable in that silence. The following are ways to encourage quiet and stillness in prayer with your children.

SCHEDULE THE TIME If possible, it is ideal for family prayer to be at a predetermined time that has been dedicated to this. Randomly trying to squeeze it into the day between homework and soccer practice, when the kids are overtired, or when they want to watch a movie does not facilitate a meaningful moment for the family. Make this a quiet time specifically reserved for prayer. Family prayer can be held at any time when everyone is together, but I prefer before bed as a way to redirect the entire day's focus back to God before going to sleep. Having children think of God right before bed helps them reorient their spirits back to their most meaningful relationship. Try to have a consistent time in your day in order to ensure that prayer is as important a ritual in the family as brushing their teeth or eating dinner.

DEDICATE THE LOCATION In order to begin this moment of talking and listening to God with your family, it is very helpful to have a dedicated space in which to pray together. This could be a particularly quiet, less distracting room in the house, it could be a bedroom, or it could be a little corner space in a room. It can be in a bed together, on a particular rug on the floor, or in any space that serves to be a tranquil place, setting the tone for the prayer. Wherever it may be, try to be consistent so that it feels like an intimate gathering place for prayer once the family congregates.

SETTING THE TONE No extra effort is needed, but some families might want extra materials to foster a feeling of prayerfulness. For instance, some families set up a little table to act as a prayer table. Children can participate in laying a linen cloth on the table, or placing a Bible or flowers. Families familiar with the Catechesis of the Good Shepherd and Montessori learning see familiar sites in the dedicated prayer spaces in the atrium, the room where the catechesis sessions are held. There, we light a candle to signal that we are about to read from the Bible, and that it is a holy time and space to prepare our hearts for the presence of God. Similarly, parents might light a candle to signal the start of prayer. Some children find looking at a candle to be a calming, soothing way to help situate their bodies and minds into a prayerful space. Additionally, some families might benefit from the playing of quiet, meditative music. Rather than add to the "noise" that we try to disengage from in prayer, quiet music can help to prepare oneself, settle down, and refocus attention.

BE FULLY PRESENT Children pick up on things quickly, and they are aware if you are wholly participating or if you are distracted. As parents, we have so much occupying our thoughts, so many things that we have to get done every day, and we have so much on our minds about tomorrow. But try to be fully present with your children in prayer. Remember that you are their primary source in their understanding of God, and they need to see your commitment and relationship with God in order for them to begin developing their own.

BE PREPARED FOR THE IMPERFECT Life with children is unpredictable, and so as much as parents plan and prepare for a nourishing and peaceful prayer service with the family, life can happen. Children can be unable to enter a place of quiet, or they can be too fidgety to calm down, or the day can be fraught with so many distractions that settling down and focusing one's attention on God just is not working. And this is okay. God is not expecting perfection, nor should you. A family prayer life should be nourishing to the family; it should fill up the soul rather than deplete it. If silence and stillness is not happening on any given night, it is okay. Listening and responding to the voice of God in prayer is a continual, life-long purpose. Don't give up, try as best as you are able, and begin again the next day.

Listening to God

As prayer is both speaking and listening to God, we not only have to teach our children the words to say, but how to listen to God as well. A peaceful silence at the beginning of a family's prayer time is an opportunity to teach our children how to listen. Getting rid of all the outside distractions and noises provides an ideal environment to hear God speak. But how do we teach our children to listen? How do they hear God's voice?

We first need to prepare our children with the knowledge that God is not always audible. To hear some individuals speak about the way God talks to them through their prayer life or the conversations they have had with God can be discouraging to many of us who may not experience God in the same way. We may not hear God speak, but we can feel God moving in our hearts and minds, directing us, and most importantly, deepening our faith. We must try to help our children understand that though we may not hear God's words, we can, through faith, continue to rely on God. God, through prayer, comforts us, heals and strengthens our spirit with wisdom, knowledge, love, and understanding of God's grace and presence in the world. We can hear and feel God's voice most clearly when we take the time to listen. God's answers to our questions are not always made clear, but prayer lets us know that God is with us, holding our hands, healing our spirits on our journey of faith. What we gain from prayer, especially through listening to God in the silence and stillness, is the ability to discern more clearly God's direction for us. Encouraging children to listen regularly to God is of paramount importance on their faith journey.

It is sometimes helpful to ask children questions to direct their thoughts during silent prayer, so as to promote "quiet" as silence with the intent to listen more clearly. Parents can ask any question that helps focus the children's attention on God and their relationship with God. The following questions/ prompts are suggestions to help guide the family's silent prayer:

"I wonder . . . " One of the most wonderful things my experience with the younger children of the Catechesis of the Good Shepherd has taught me is to cultivate a sense of wonder of God in the children. By responding to a Bible story or a child's question with, "I wonder . . . ," and letting our voice fade away as we look up and away in thought, the children see this and often try to imitate it. This encourages them to contemplate and organize questions of faith on their own. Being a catechist or a parent is not merely about giving our children answers to every question or imparting our knowledge unto them, but to encourage them to puzzle and think about these spiritual matters in their own way. This awakens a sense of wonder and insight in the spiritual being of the child that goes well beyond that of any formal catechesis or traditional theology. So, for instance, at the beginning of a family prayer, a parent might say, "I wonder where I felt God most today . . . " and then remain silent for a few minutes as the rest of the family contemplates this statement. If something wonderful happened that day—or something sad—the statement might be "I wonder where God was today when _____ happened . . ." The answers never have to be verbalized, yet they prompt the children to begin thinking and listening to God.

When was I happiest today? When did I make others happiest? When was I closest to God? Encouraging children to relate happiness of spirit and closeness to God is to help them evaluate their day according to their relationship with God. It helps them understand on a basic level the connectedness of life and faith. Spending a few minutes thinking about this helps them to center themselves to God.

Where did I see Jesus today? This question helps children reimagine their day in context of relationships. Remembering that God is always present in the world and acting all around us helps children to see their day through the lens of faith.

The first movement of a family prayer ritual is to center the family in a moment of silence and stillness. This can take a minute, or several, but it encourages the family to settle down in a peaceful space and refocus the family's attention on God and faith. It demands that prayer become more than just talking to God, but that we also listen to God's voice and presence. It is perhaps the most difficult part of any prayer—preparing our hearts in such a way that we can hear God communicating with us. To be in mutual relationship with God is to acknowledge that we are, at times, to be still and to listen in the silence.

Reflection Questions and Suggestions

Gather your children today for prayer, and ask them to close their eyes, keep their bodies still, and listen closely to God. Begin with only a few moments, but build on the time as your family continues to practice.

Ask your children what they heard when they were listening to God.

Can you add anything to your prayer space to set the tone for a peaceful silence? Consider candles, dimming the lights, flowers, etc.

Help your children attain a peaceful silence by asking them questions about their day and their relationship with God. Allow them time to contemplate on the answers.

- ❀ **When were you happiest today?**

- ❀ **When did you make others happy?**

- ❀ **When did you feel closest to God?**

- ❀ **When did you feel far away from God?**

- ❀ **Where did you see Jesus acting today?**

Sharing Prayers of Gratitude

I will give thanks to you, O Lord,
among the peoples,
And I will sing praises to you
among the nations.
For your steadfast love is higher
than the heavens,
And your faithfulness reaches to the clouds.

—Psalm 108:3–4

Prayers of thanksgiving invoke a spirit of gratitude for all God's wondrous deeds, for God's many blessings, and for simply being. We are thankful for God's faithfulness and love, and most importantly, for God's continued presence in our lives. All things come from God. When we receive something, we respond with a grateful heart. We want to instill in our children this gratitude, and to respond to God in prayer.

A family prayer ritual should include prayers of gratitude. After gathering together, and centering your hearts and spirits, move towards giving thanks to God for the day. It can be as simple as "Thank you Jesus for this day!" or as complex as going around to each member to say specifically what they are thankful for most on that day. We need to acknowledge that God is acting in our lives, and we are thankful for that presence.

Understanding Gratitude

Generally speaking, it is fairly easy to teach kids to say thank you. As parents, we teach them that when they receive something, or someone does something kind for them, we respond with a "thank you." When someone shares their favorite crayon or toys, lets them take a turn jumping rope, or puts a plate of food in front of them, children are able to say "thanks" without too much trouble. Usually, with modeling a quick "thank you," frequent repetition, and quiet reminders, children are pretty quick to understand that when they receive, they give thanks. It becomes habitual in nature.

It is easy to say thank you, and fairly easy to more or less train our children to say thanks out of politeness, pleasantry, and good manners. It is more difficult, however, to teach our children *gratitude as relationship*. Gratitude is our response for all that God has done for us. "O give thanks to the Lord, for he is good; for his steadfast love endures forever" (Psalm 107:1). Through his goodness God has created us and continues to sustain us.

Genuine gratitude turns what we have into *enough* when we realize that its one true source is God. We are content and fulfilled knowing that God has blessed us and will continue to sustain us; we are thankful for God's presence and everlasting commitment to us. Gratitude brings us contentment in God and God alone. St. Paul writes to the Philippians:

Not that I am referring to being in need; for I have learned to be content with whatever I have. I know what it is to have little, and I know what it is to have plenty. In any and all circumstances I have learned the secret of being well-fed and of going hungry, of having plenty and of being in need. I can do all things through him who strengthens me.

—4:11–13

Gratitude is not simply being thankful for something but is the recognition that everything comes from God. The Gospel of Luke tells the story of Jesus cleansing the ten lepers:

On the way to Jerusalem Jesus was going through the region between Samaria and Galilee. As he entered a village, ten lepers approached him. Keeping their distance, they called out, saying, "Jesus, Master, have mercy on us!" When he saw them, he said to them, "Go and show yourselves to the priests." And as they went, they were made clean. Then one of them, when he saw that he was healed, turned back, praising God with a loud voice. He prostrated himself at Jesus' feet and thanked him. And he was a Samaritan. Then Jesus asked, "Were not ten made clean? But the other nine, where are they? Was none of them found to return and give praise to God except this foreigner?" Then he said to him, "Get up and go on your way; your faith has made you well."

—17:11–19

Jesus gives us much and deserves our thankfulness. Gratitude involves stopping and thinking where God has been in our lives, how God is acting, and responding with a prayer of thanks.

Gratitude in Family Prayer

An important distinction that all parents might understand is that being grateful involves more than an obligatory thank you. True gratitude digs deeper into recognizing all things come from God, and this is a more difficult concept for children to comprehend. Nevertheless, it is essential to sow the seeds of a grateful heart in the lives of our children. We can begin with the basics, and build our way up to a more comprehensive understanding of gratitude:

BEGIN WITH THANKFULNESS We must encourage our children to respond with thankfulness when they receive any gift. Gratefulness is not simply about the things we receive but the relationship that is present. Thankfulness is appropriate in all moments in our day. This is especially appropriate on our everyday moments of prayer, including our prayer walks.

THANKFULNESS FOR PRESENCE Introduce the notion of being thankful for the time someone spends with you, for being with you and being present in their day, whether it be a friend, neighbor, teacher, or family member. Focus on saying thank you for the moments you have together rather than for the things you receive from that person.

THANK GOD It is so important to specifically and clearly thank God for being with us, every day. Take a moment and thank God not just for the things we receive, but just simply for being present. It can be a simple, "Thank you God for being with us on this day." Thank God, frequently and repeatedly with your children, just for being God.

THANK GOD FOR GIFTS Thank God for all God's gifts that we have in abundance: food, water, nature, light, day, etc. Recognize again that all these things come from God.

THANK GOD FOR SPIRITUAL GIFTS Focus some time thanking God for the more spiritual of gifts of wisdom, knowledge, faith, healing, miracles, prophecy, strength, compassion, etc. These are not necessarily tangible, but nevertheless are gifts from God.

In the context of family prayer time, ask your children what they might want to thank God for that day. Prompt them as necessary, asking questions to encourage them. Perhaps each member can add in prayer the thing or person that they are most thankful for that day. Regularly include prayer to thank God for being with us daily, for though we can be thankful for the things we receive, the experiences we have, and the people in our lives, we are most thankful for the continued presence of and relationship with God.

Reflection Questions and Suggestions

- ❀ **Where was God today in your life?**
- ❀ **What are you most thankful for today?**
- ❀ **Who are you most thankful for today?**
- ❀ **What gifts did you receive from God today?**
- ❀ **What spiritual gifts did you receive from God?**
- ❀ **What can we say to God for these gifts?**

6 Interceding for Others

$\mathcal{A}t$ the close of the session in the Catechesis of the Good Shepherd, the children gather for communal prayer. Each week, the children take turns preparing, usually with a partner, the prayer service for the rest of their small community of friends and catechists. Each and every week, the children choose to include a time for intercessions. The children share a prayer they have for another, and we all respond with "Lord, hear our prayer." When my children were in the Catechesis of the Good Shepherd, three things would happen each week, without fail.

First, on the way home from catechesis, my children would share with me who or what they prayed for and why. For instance, they would pray for a friend at school because they were injured on the playground. Or they would pray for their Grandpa because he was sick. And we would talk about it a little more, and they would share with me their worries. These were not thoughts that they had shared with me prior to Catechesis, but subjects they had brought up on their own during the course of their communal prayers.

Secondly, my children shared with me several of the prayers of the other children in their atrium, prayers that really made an impression on them, and they shared not only their friends' concerns, but also what had now become their own concerns. Listening to them speak, I heard compassion, empathy, and concern for those they were praying for.

And lastly, during my time as catechist, I noticed that as one child prayed for something, it would lead another child to pray for something similar that related to them in their own lives. For instance, one child would pray for an area in the world that had just suffered from an earthquake. Then another child would pray for flooding that was happening in another part of the world. And then yet another would pray for an area that was experiencing extreme drought. Or one child would pray for their aunt who learned she had cancer. Following that, there would be prayers for a grandma who was sick or an uncle who just had surgery.

Prayers of intercession were consistently the longest portion of our weekly communal prayer. Frequently, the catechists would eventually have to move on without every prayer being said because there simply was not enough time. The children always had prayers that they wished to say and bring to our little community. They were genuine, heartfelt prayers filled with concerns and needs that were in their hearts. Sharing their worries and concerns with their little community of friends brought them comfort and healing. Frequently, one of the children would remember a prayer from the previous week and ask how an aunt or friend was doing. They were building relationships with God, to whom they prayed and lifted up their worries, but they also created a small community who shared in their needs and cares.

Intercessions are a type of prayer that not only brings us closer to God, but brings us closer to each other and to the larger community. Encouraging prayers of intercession with our children helps them to understand the interconnectedness of their home with the larger faith community, and with the world. Intercessions do so much for the larger church community, allowing a visible sign that we are many members, but one body in Christ, and that "If one member suffers, all suffer together with it; if one member is honored, all rejoice together with it" (1 Corinthians 12:12, 26). Including intercessions as a moment of your family prayer allows us to do the following:

Introduce the Mass into Your Home

The Prayer of the Faithful, Universal Prayer, or General Intercessions is where our Catholic community prays for others during the Mass. Some Church communities provide time for members of the community to share their needs and burdens in front of all so that the community might lift them up together in prayer. These are not one-time prayers that end with the Mass, but rather, prayers that members take home and continue to pray regularly. We also share in intercessions, prayers of thanksgiving, and petitions of our own so that we become one body in Christ, united in love and spirit. In general, the prayers of intercession during the Mass fall under one of the following categories:

- needs of the Church

- needs of the whole world, including Church and world leaders

- those peoples or individuals suffering or burdened

- needs of the local community

During intercessions, the faithful come together in one voice and pray to God. It is a moment of interconnectivity and togetherness through prayer that is vital to the identity of the Church. It can also be vital to the identity of the family in that it can designate your family as one that looks *outward* and recognizes that the Church is participating in the body of Christ globally.

Bringing a part of the Mass into your homes recognizes that your household is a domestic church, and that the domestic church is not *less than* the parish church, but is rather an extension of it in the way of faith, hope, love, and community. Participating in the Church at home through intercessions allows both family members and church members to feel the children's contribution to the prayer life of the Church. Children are members of the community of believers, and they need to participate in that community in the church and at home.

Listen to Our Children's Hearts

As you begin your prayer journey with your children, we need to help our children bridge the gap between talking about God and praying to God. Whereas younger children can do this more fluidly, older children have a more difficult time, whether it is the difficulty of finding the words, or the embarrassment or uncomfortableness of praying out loud, or just the uncertainty of how to even begin. Most children, I believe, find praying for others less difficult. During my time with the Catechesis of the Good Shepherd, I have found that with regular exposure and practice, and a safe space to do it in, even the quietest of children will eventually find the words to pray for something or someone in the presence of their peers. Prayer provides an outlet for our children to speak their hearts in a way that simply talking might not. Intercessory prayers at home allow parents to witness the innermost feelings, needs, and concerns of our children. It provides a mode of communication that allows us to see into the heart and soul of our children.

Communicating their concerns to God also allows our children to communicate with us. God knows our thoughts and our hearts without us needing to verbalize them. But sometimes we need help in understanding our children's fears, worries, or concerns. Encouraging our children to verbalize their thoughts through prayers of petition and intercession allows us to glimpse a piece of them that we might not otherwise have an opportunity to see. We can use these moments as a gateway to future discussion and communicate individually with our children—not to spy on them, but to understand our children more deeply.

Instill an Understanding of Social Justice

Praying for others allows both parents and children to move outside their own worldview. In praying for someone else's needs, children may begin to understand the works of God as justice and mercy. Through praying for another, we begin to understand the commandment "Love your neighbor as yourself" and the parable of the Good Samaritan. We are called to "bear one another's burdens" and to "love one another as I have loved you" (Galatians 6:2, John 15:12).

To pray for another is to understand that we share, through God, our struggles, worries, hurts, needs, and desires. We might not be able to fix these burdens, or even know how to help. But we can begin with our children to create an awareness that we are all connected, and the needs of others are our own. Praying for these needs with our children recognizes the interconnectedness of all of God's creations and plants the seeds of social justice.

Prayer as a Call to Action

Furthering the call to social justice, we acknowledge through prayer that once we are aware of the needs of others, we are called to help them. Prayer offers our children the opportunity to begin the works of justice. The prophet Micah says,

> He has told you, O mortal, what is good;
> and what does the Lord require of you
> but to do justice, and to love kindness,
> and to walk humbly with your God?
>
> —6:8

Justice is an *action*; it is something we do. Justice is a behavior in relationship with others and with God. Acknowledging the needs of others through intercessory prayer is to ask God for greater peace through justice in our world.

Proverbs tells us, "Speak out for those who cannot speak, for the rights of all the destitute. Speak out, judge righteously, defend the rights of the poor and needy" (31:8–9). Social ministry begins, and is anchored, in prayer. It is there we can understand God's call to seek justice and begin to pursue peace. Through intercessory prayer, we can pray for all people who experience injustice and for those who cause injustice; we can pray that people in power might enact change, that the local and worldwide communities might work together for change, and that our Church community might lead the response to justice.

Intercessory prayer links us to the needs of the rest of the world. In understanding the needs of others, and praying for those needs, we begin a conversation on the works of mercy and justice. Beginning this conversation early with children is to have them grow socially aware and recognize that only through God can peace and justice be realized.

Prayers of Intercession in the Home

After meeting together in peaceful silence and sharing in prayers of gratitude, the family can begin prayers of intercession. As with prayers of gratitude, these are meant to be spontaneous prayers. If your children are having a hard time verbalizing what is on their hearts or don't know where to begin, it is okay to offer some prompts or questions to help them or to model these prayers by beginning first. Some days the children might have many prayers to say, and other days, just a few. Do not force a child to pray aloud, but a moment or two of additional silence might encourage them to begin. Being consistent in offering times of intercessory prayers will help your children pray more frequently and with ease.

It is helpful to begin with a small and intimate worldview and move towards the larger world (though spontaneous prayer, of course, is not meant to be organized, it is crucial that our children learn that we can pray for both those near and close to us and those far away that we do not know). The following are some guidelines for family intercessions. You need not include all of these at every prayer time; they are more for understanding how we might encourage our children to pray in a way that develops a moral ethic.

1. Begin with the prayers that are on each of your hearts individually, and the needs of your small family unit.

2. Pray for the needs of your family members and friends.

3. Pray for the needs of your Church.

4. Pray for the needs of the larger, local community.

5. Pray for worldwide needs.

6. Remember especially to lift up a prayer for social justice, including peace and justice in the world, the needs of the poor and vulnerable, human rights, dignity of all, and care for the earth.

7. Include another moment of silent prayer for those prayers still in our hearts that we might not be able to verbalize.

8. After each prayer, respond as a family as we do in Mass, "Lord, hear our prayer."

I believe that once your family is in the habit of praying together, you will find that prayers of intercession will take some time. Children have a way of opening their hearts to the needs of others that we as parents might do well to mimic. Sharing our concerns for others with our families unites us in a very real and deeply spiritual way. Praying together nurtures our compassion for others while bringing us comfort in knowing there are people sharing in our sorrows and needs. Furthermore, prayers of intercession expand our worldview to include peoples and areas outside our realm of closeness, broadening our moral ethic to include others outside our immediate proximity. Acknowledging that we are social beings with communal needs and responsibilities, intercessory prayers allow us to identify injustices, gather courage and strength, and answer the call to follow Jesus in the ways of justice and peace, so that

> Steadfast love and faithfulness will meet;
> Righteousness and peace will kiss each other.
> Faithfulness will spring up from the ground,
> And righteousness will look down from the sky.
> —Psalms 85:10–11

Reflection Questions and Suggestions

- ❀ **Who is God leading you to pray for?**

- ❀ **How did God answer you?**

- ❀ **Remember to thank God.**

- ❀ **What can we do for others this week?**

- ❀ **Who is close to us that could use our prayers?**

- ❀ **What is happening in the world that needs our prayers?**

Use songs or Bible passages to highlight the call for justice and peace (e.g., "Let There Be Peace on Earth")

7 Reflections and Conversations

Inevitable in raising children in the Catholic faith is the knowledge that at some point, your children are going to ask you a question about God to which you won't have the answer. Some of us will at least have our children in religious education or catechesis before that happens, so we can say, "Hmmm. . . . I don't know; maybe you should ask (name of catechist) this week?" The rest of us have to somehow come up with an answer or figure it out, lest our children think we know nothing and we start wishing there was a manual for this sort of thing.

Raising inquisitive children in our Church brings about a lot of questions. When my oldest was seven and learning about the Passover meal, she wanted to know about everything Passover. Or when my then three-year-old was fixated on Jesus' beard and asked, "Are you sure he had a beard, Mama?" Or when my young son, after finding a bouncy ball inside an egg during an Easter egg hunt with the phrase "God's Greatest Gift" on it, argued with his siblings that a bouncy ball was, indeed, God's greatest gift *because it said so,* while his sister argued that it was an elephant, and they both turned to me, eager to prove each other wrong, "Mama, What is God's greatest gift?" Or when learning the history of the Kingdom of God in Catechesis of the Good Shepherd, my daughter asked me, "What exactly was God doing before the first day of creation?"

Whether or not these are all deeply theological questions that deserve an equally deep theological answer is beside the point. Our children have questions—so many questions— about God, Jesus, Church, Mass, the Bible, and everything in between. Even with two theology degrees, I have many a time been left speechless by my children—bewildered and wholly at a loss not only by their less theological questions (e.g., the bouncy ball), but also by their insightful questions that get down to the meaning of what it is to be a follower of Jesus. Their questions can leave me questioning how exactly to *begin* to answer, and wondering who exactly had the theological background.

Children have questions about their faith. Encourage their questions and their desire to understand their faith. Create a safe home environment in which all questions are treated with respect and great care. Questions mean that faith is active and alive in your child's heads and hearts—they are just trying to make sense of it all. Children really are little theologians. Our job as parents is to lead them and hope that they will follow.

These questions—whether they be the deep theological questions that we adults still struggle with, or the simple, sometimes humorous, questions befitting of children trying to work their minds around something—are important in that they first, and foremost, keep their worldview centered around their faith. It keeps them talking, thinking, and wondering about God and God's role in their lives. Secondly, our answers, though perhaps sometimes simplistic, help our children form a larger pattern in their minds that shape their comprehensive understanding of God. Each little piece of information that they retain, decipher, and understand helps build their consciousness of God.

Finally, children are inquisitive. If we are not prepared to at least attempt to answer their questions, they will seek their answers elsewhere. It is incredibly important that our children know we are a source to come to when they are pondering those big questions of faith and life. How can we, as parents and as our children's first and primary catechists, encourage our children to ask these questions, to continue on their journey to understanding God, and thereby who they are?

BE OPEN ABOUT YOUR UNDERSTANDING OF GOD. If there ever was a time to be honest and fully open in your beliefs about God, talking with your children is it. Don't try to give perfect textbook answers—your children will see through that and hear the insincerity. Be truthful about what you know, what you don't know, and what you believe. They need to know, too, that faith is a lifelong journey, that though you might not have the answers, you still depend on God.

IT'S LESS ABOUT THE ANSWERS THAN IT IS ABOUT THE QUESTIONS. When our children ask us questions about God, it's because they are trying to figure out their faith and God. To ask questions is a sign of faith. It's when we stop asking, stop discerning God's role in our lives, that our faith lessens. Encourage your children to talk and ask about God, and show them that you, too, are still seeking answers.

ENCOURAGE YOUR CHILDREN TO PARTICIPATE. Helping your children to become more involved in your church, your catechesis program, and various groups within your church, surrounds them with a community of similarly minded children filled with curiosity, questions, and desire to find answers. Participating in church activities with similarly inquisitive children provides them with a built-in community through which they can continue to be inspired to ask questions. Providing them with a community of their own encourages them to remain invested and active in their own faith journey. As they become more involved, they will have more questions, but they will also be able to share their questions among their own community.

SHOW THEM THAT YOU PARTICIPATE. When your children see that you are involved, that your faith is more than attending church on Sundays, they become aware that faith accompanies their entire life. To demonstrate that you are still on your faith journey, that you have your own community of faith, is to show that belief in God and commitment to your church is a lifelong endeavor. Furthermore, to show your children that you still have questions, and are constantly striving to understand your faith, is to help your children comprehend that not having answers is part of what *faith* means—"confidence of things hoped for, the conviction of things not seen" (Hebrews 11:1).

But how do we actually respond to those questions that our children bring to us?

WITH AN ANSWER. If you know the answer, share it!

ASK THEM WHAT THEY THINK. Just as catechists in the Catechesis of the Good Shepherd often respond with "I wonder," it is particularly helpful to ask the children to answer their own question. It allows them to ponder aloud, to verbalize their thought process, in the hopes that they might come to a satisfactory answer on their own. Whether or not you as parents know the answer is beside the point. Allowing our children to work through their own faith in the safety of our home is a great gift.

FOCUS ON THEMES OF OUR FAITH RATHER THAN ON A SPECIFIC ANSWER. Rather than giving a theologically sound answer to a puzzling question, it is easier—and often more helpful—to focus on the larger meaning of faith that shapes our understanding of God, Christianity, and Scripture.

FIND THE ANSWER TOGETHER. If focusing on the themes of faith is not enough, or your children are insistent on finding an answer, show your children that you are willing to be invested in their faith by helping them find their answer, whether by asking someone, looking it up online, or reading the Bible together. Don't dismiss their questions as being unimportant or ridiculous. Help them through their questions, and let them know that their faith is important.

ENCOURAGE THEM TO SEEK THE ANSWERS. Encourage them to talk to a catechist, your parish priest, or someone they would recognize as being part of your community. Besides helping them discover answers, this connects them to members of their faith and builds relationships. It will let them know that there are so many individuals invested in their lives and journey.

Reflection and Conversation in Family Prayer

We are meant to talk about God with our children whenever possible. When your children come to you with questions, talk about God. When you find grace in an ordinary moment of life, talk about God. When questions about Jesus come up during dinner, talk them through. When there is a major world disaster, talk about where God is in that situation. When your children come to you with joy, talk about God. Just as God can be part of our everyday life, we can also talk about God in our family prayer life. Less a "stage" of prayer than an understanding that you are meant to talk about God whenever possible, it is nevertheless important to carve out specific times to simply talk about God. If questions arise about God from your children, family prayer time is an ideal moment to bring up these questions and talk about God. Prayer can be a safe space into which your children can bring their questions about God and faith, so that you and your family might discuss God in any way. Faith is deepened through questioning and understanding God's place in your life. Encourage your children to bring their questions to your family prayer.

It is also a time where you as parents can ask your children questions as to how God is working in their lives. Knowing that God is present in their lives is one thing, but to understand that God is moving through their lives, directing and leading them, is another. Help them discern where God is present in their lives by asking them where they feel God most throughout their day.

Intrinsic to our Catholic moral ethic is that our faith is to visibly direct our actions in a way that shapes both who we are and how we are to act and live in this world. Family prayer time is an appropriate moment to ask each of your family members where God is working in their lives. Your children may have many things to say, or they may be stuck and unsure. In the Catechesis of the Good Shepherd, one of the ways that impacted my children the most was focusing on maxims. Maxims are words and phrases that Jesus said in the New Testament that give us an understanding of how we are to live—the beginnings of a moral ethic. For instance:

> I give you a new commandment: Love one another as I have loved you.
> —John 13:34

> I do not say forgive seven times, but seventy times seven.
> —Matthew 5:37

> Love your enemies.
> —Matthew 5:44

> Ask, and you will receive. Seek, and you will find. Knock, and the door will be opened.
> —Matthew 7:7

My children would pick a maxim during their catechesis session, write it down, bring it home, put it by their beds, and read it daily, pondering its meaning and place in their lives. Some days, they would come home from school and say, "I know exactly what my maxim means!" And they would share with me something that happened at school that really spoke to them and helped them understand what Jesus said. Other times, they were unsure and would struggle and not really comprehend the meaning. When that happened, they would find comfort in either talking about it, continuing to contemplate it, or bringing it to their friends in catechesis and discussing it further. Discussing these maxims outside of church and Catechesis created an atmosphere of learning and contemplation about God. Living as Jesus asks is not a simple thing. It takes effort and struggle, but it is something we strive for as a family.

During family prayer, it is important to carve out a moment to discuss God in our lives. After gathering with a peaceful silence, saying prayers of gratitude, and intercessions, it is beneficial to take the time for reflection and conversation. This can be as simple as talking to your kids about where God is acting in their life, or asking them if they have any questions about God or their faith, but it can also be a time to have a conversation about recognizing God in their lives, about their struggles in understanding God, or to discuss what it means to be a follower of Jesus in the everyday. Perhaps you can pick a maxim or Bible story to discuss throughout the week, or you can use life's events to narrate the conversation for the day. An open and frequent dialogue must exist for children to develop their theological, spiritual, and ethical selves.

Reflection Questions and Suggestions

Pick a maxim or passage from the Bible that might particularly pertain to your daily life. Read it and discuss:

- ❀ **What did it mean to them?**

- ❀ **How did it apply in their lives?**

- ❀ **How does it help them make decisions?**

- ❀ **What does the maxim tell us about Jesus?**

- ❀ **Are maxims hard or easy to follow?**

What do you remember about Mass this week?

Where was God in your day?

When did you feel God with you the most? When were you happiest?

When were you lonely or did not feel God's presence?

Is it easy following Jesus?

Ask your children what questions they have about God, church, or the Bible.

How might you develop your own faith and understanding of God, Church, or the Bible?

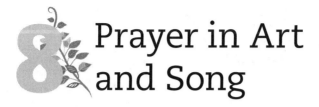

Prayer in Art and Song

My family loves to sing. We may not have the best voices, and we may not carry a tune as well as some, but we love to sing. Walking into my children's rooms every morning, I would sing a song from an old Bible songs for kids cassette tape that was on repeat when I was younger, until my children started singing with me. That usually started their day with a smile. We would sing a song of thanksgiving before meals, and sometimes during meals. If we heard a new song at church that week, we would sing it all week. My children would randomly pick a song out of an old church hymnal, and we would sing that at our family prayer time in the evenings. Usually, they dragged out bedtime for "just one more song, please!" and we would sing until my voice started cracking and I would finally have to really mean it that it was time for bed. Music, especially church music, was definitely part of my childhood as well, so much so that my parents finally implemented a rule that there was to be no singing at the dinner table or you had to do dishes, else we sat there for hours, singing and laughing, and definitely not eating our vegetables.

My youngest daughter used to love to make "books" about everything and anything related to God or church. She wrote a very heavily sized tome detailing everything there is to know about catechesis, an instructional guide to Sunday liturgy, a prayer book with every prayer that she could remember—correct words or no—and a guide to the liturgical seasons, amongst others. My oldest worked incredibly hard, week after week, on her own copy of the History of the Kingdom of Salvation materials in the Catechesis of the Good Shepherd, which included a timeline of all major moments of creation and redemption from Genesis to today. And my middle child was so interested in the presentation of the gifts of God in Catechesis that he would collect rocks, plants, and other pieces of nature and start his own collection. All of these items—homemade books, guides, artwork, and collections that become part of your children's spiritual understanding, can be part of your prayer life as well.

Prayer isn't meant to have a static, dull, unchanging presence. It should be full of nourishment for our souls and be both life-giving and life-changing. It should be a source of strength for us, deepening our relationship with God and each other. In order for prayer to be all of these things, it needs to *become part of our very being*, not something we have to do—just another check off of our long schedule for the day. When we are not just saying a prayer, but creating it and living it, prayer becomes a relationship that we cannot go without—it is sustaining us.

As you continue on your prayer journey with your family, one way to enrich your habitual family prayer is to include other sources of spiritual insight into your prayer. While this part of prayer is something that you as parent can organize and develop, I would suggest that this is an area that can really help your children to become involved. For example, ask to bring something that they are interested in to the time of prayer. It may be an area of interest at school or other activity in which they are involved. Your children's interests and gifts can enhance your family's prayer time but making it a unique, welcoming, spiritual time for your family. I encourage you to add to your family prayer any material that enriches your prayer and allows your relationship with your children and God to strengthen and become more life giving. The following are some ways to include other sources or mediums of spiritual insight into your family prayer.

BIBLE VERSES AND READINGS Children hear Bible readings every Sunday at Mass, but they sometimes have a hard time following along. Help your children become more comfortable with hearing God's Word by including either Bible readings or verses into your prayer time. These can be taken from the appropriate daily readings according to our liturgical calendar, or they can be just passages, maxims, stories, parables, or verses that you might want to include that day. Your children can help pick these out, or you can pick them out for your family. If your

The answer came, "the one who treated him whith compassion."

Jesus Said to him, "then go and do the same."

Luke 10:30-37

children are interested in a particular story, read that, even if you find yourself coming back to the same stories. Familiarity with the Bible, even in small pieces, can help your children understand overall themes and patterns.

ARTWORK Enrich your worship space by using artwork, paintings or drawings, either made by your children or from a book, online, or from another artifact. Place these in your prayer place, either to enhance your space or to include as something to look at or talk about during your prayer. If your children want to become even more involved with certain Biblical passages, have them copy the words, or draw a photo to enrich your prayer, just as murals, statues, and other works are used in our churches.

COLLECTIONS OR OTHER MATERIALS Some children like to use objects, like flowers, rocks, shells, or leaves, as a visible sign of God's creation. Place these on a table near your prayer space to visibly include them in your prayer. These pieces can bring some children to God's presence, especially if they are involved in the collection and creating of the space.

SONGS Those who sing pray twice! Some families are not musical, and that is okay. Music can still be part of your prayer time. Some like church music, or Christian radio, or classical, or mainstream music that speaks to them about God and their faith. Soft music can set the tone for a prayerful silence, while a song of praise can be used in prayers of gratitude. The Psalms tell us to sing songs of praise and to shout joyfully to God! Open your home to these songs of praise, and encourage your children to proclaim their love of God with all their hearts!

STORIES OF SAINTS OR BIBLE CHARACTERS Prayer time is a wonderful moment to include stories of our tradition's saints or various Bible characters. Use children's books or the

Internet to supplement and teach your children about historical people of faith. My children would want to hear the story of Esther repeatedly when they were younger, and we taught them the stories of St. Lucy and St. Nicholas during the winter months.

PRAYERS Include other prayers that you may have heard, read, or discovered in your prayer. These can be traditional prayers that you have heard in Mass, like the Our Father or Glory Be, or they can be prayers that you have heard or read from other literature. Your children can be another source of these prayers. Help them to create prayers that mean something to your family, or read a prayer that they have written.

LITURGICAL SEASON Pay attention to the liturgical season—and natural seasons—and include materials or prayers relevant to the time of year that the church is celebrating. For instance, place an item that represents the gifts you receive from God during Advent (rather than focusing on the gifts we get under the tree), or place lilies, eggs, or items that represent new life during Easter. During Thanksgiving, create a list of things you are thankful for and place it in your prayer space.

All of these items are ways to create a family prayer time that will be uniquely individualized for the needs of your family. I encourage you to include songs, prayers, or spiritual items that have meaning for your family. Adding these elements to your prayer speaks to where your family is at any moment. Create an atmosphere that is life-giving, enriching, and incorporates all that makes your family *yours*. Prayer shouldn't be something that *has* to get done, it should be a moment in your busy lives where you all *want* to be, that connects you to each other and your whole purpose—life in God.

Include as many forms of prayer as time and space allow. Encourage your children to be involved—at all ages. The more they are involved, the longer they will stay involved, and carry out these moments in their future lives. These other forms of prayer allow for different learning needs and spiritual needs of your children. Some children learn a great deal from Sunday Mass—they are able to follow along and pay attention from an early age. Others have a hard time sitting still and need a more involved, tactile method of prayer in order to keep their attention and focus. Including these other forms of prayer allow for these differences and speak to a wider spectrum of children. It enables prayer to be real, something they can touch and be a physical part of creating. It allows for creativity and imagination to be a part of your prayer life—so important for the spiritual development of many children and adults.

Prayer time should speak to who you are as a family, and your children should be a big part of that. They should rightfully feel that they are integral to your prayer—they should take ownership and feel that prayer is an important part of your family's life together. Including other mediums in your family prayer is a way for your children to take a leadership role in their spiritual life. Let them pick out a Bible story, or a song, or have them draw pictures or write a prayer to include. Help your children take creative control—let them include materials that mean something in their relationship with God, and most importantly, let your children tell you about it. Prayer time is not simply a two-way conversation with your family and God, it's also an important time to both talk to *and listen* to your children. Let them tell you about their faith—which prayers they like, why they wrote a prayer, what songs they love, why they drew a particular picture, what Bible stories they're learning about, why they want to include shells in your prayer space, etc. Let them tell you so that you might understand where they are at in their spiritual journey, but so that they might also *teach you* on your journey, if you are listening closely.

Reflection Questions and Suggestions

Ask your children if they would like to decorate your prayer space. Help them to create a place to pray.

Chose a biblical character or a saint to learn about for the week as a family.

Is there a piece of art that your children would like to create to enrich your prayer?

Ask your children to remember a song from church and sing it together.

Start a prayer journal with your family.

Consider the current liturgical season and the natural season in your prayer. What can you add to your prayer during each season? Consider the following as well as other major holidays:

Liturgical Seasons

- ❀ **Advent**
- ❀ **Christmas**
- ❀ **Lent**
- ❀ **Triduum**
- ❀ **Easter**

Natural Seasons

- ❀ **Spring**
- ❀ **Summer**
- ❀ **Fall**
- ❀ **Winter**

Civic and Cultural days

- ❀ **New Year's Day**
- ❀ **Martin Luther King Jr.'s Day**
- ❀ **Valentine's Day**
- ❀ **President's Day**
- ❀ **Independence Day**
- ❀ **Labor Day**
- ❀ **Thanksgiving**

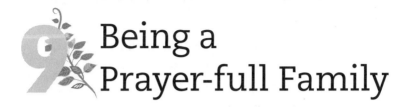

Being a Prayer-full Family

a perfect, full day of family prayer might include:

Waking your children up and offering a prayer of praise for the day.

> We praise you and give you glory for this day!
> Glory to God in the Highest!

Giving thanks for the morning meal.

> Bless us, O Lord,
> And these, thy gifts,
> Which we are about to receive
> From thy bounty,
> Through Christ, our Lord.
> Amen.

Praying together before everyone heads off into their day, orienting the family to Jesus.

> Jesus,
> Be on my mind,
> On my lips,
> And in my heart.

Encouraging your children to see God around us, and responding to God with prayer.

> Thank you, God, for all your beautiful
> gifts of creation.
> Thank you for providing us with
> trees for shade to read under.
> Thank you for the sun to brighten our days.
> Thank you for being in the rain and
> nourishing the earth.

Helping our children to call out to God, whether they are happy or hurting.

> Thank you Jesus for being near me!
>
> Be with me, Lord. Comfort me.

Praying for our friends when they are hurting.

> Be with my friends when they are sad, Jesus.
> Help them to feel better.

Praying together on the way home from school.

> Lord God, thank you for our teachers and our
> friends. Help us to remember all we have learned.

Praying before dinner.

> We thank you for the food we eat,
> We thank you for the friends we meet.
> We thank you for the sun above,
> We thank you for your love.

We gather together in prayer and rest a moment in a peaceful silence, wondering at the ways you are at work in our lives. We share our gratitude for God's presence in our day.

> Thank you for being with us today.
> Thank you for helping me when I needed you.
> Thank you for being with me when I was afraid.
> Thank you for giving me the strength I needed today.

We pray for others who are in need.

> For our Grandma, that she may heal.
> > Lord, hear our prayer.
> For our church, that we can heal our community.
> > Lord, hear our prayer.
> For all those that are homeless and who hunger.
> > Lord, hear our prayer.

We talk about how God has worked in our lives today.

> I wonder when we were happiest today. Did we feel God there?
>
> Jesus said to love our enemies. Did we not get along with someone today? How did we respond?

We sing together our favorite psalms and songs from church.

> *Alleluia, Alleluia, Alleluia, Alleluia!*

We pray the Glory Be together.

> Glory be to the Father,
> and to the Son,
> and to the Holy Spirit,
> As it was in the beginning,
> is now, and ever shall be,
> world without end. Amen.

And then our day will have ended, and we go to sleep, only to wake up and begin all over again in the morning. But sometimes life happens. And our lives are, by no means, perfect. Kids get antsy and wiggly. Spouses work late and are out of town. There are after school activities and sports, dinner, homework, and bathing. Adults work late and have various household chores to do. Some children get grouchy long before bedtime, some get a surge of energy late at night, and some fall asleep early. And sometimes our hearts are closed off, and we fail to feel the presence of God. Parenting is hard. We are exhausted and stressed, and never seem to have enough hours in the day. We don't remember to pray before meals because we are lucky if we manage to make the meals. The older our children get, the longer our days get. How do we become the family that prays together, so that we might stay together? How can all of this be done? Is it a little ambitious for even the most time-blessed families? Families are messy, imperfect, full of good intentions, but often with too little time, energy, and follow through. And that is okay. Keep in mind the following on your family's prayer journey:

- There is no wrong way to pray! There are no time limitations or word minimums for prayer, nor are there right or wrong words. Pray however you know how, with whatever words you have, with whatever amount of time you have—but pray! Pray with your heart, and that is enough!

- Pray when you can and where you can, but pray often and teach your children to do the same. Show them that you pray, and *pray without ceasing!*

- *Teaching* your children to pray can only go so far. *Showing* them that *you* pray can be everything.

- Do what you can, when you can. Something is always better than nothing. A one-minute, quick prayer where you are fully present and resting in the presence of the Lord is better than a fifteen-minute prayer where you are making mental to-do lists rather than concentrating on your relationship with God. Be present in prayer, especially when with your children.

- Family prayer takes practice. Just like everything in a family, a prayer life is not perfect, and that is okay. Begin again the next day.

- If anything, begin your day with a prayer, whether it is in bed or at breakfast. Start your family's day in prayer.

- Start simple—look for those prayerful moments.

- Remember that your children are never too young to pray, nor are they ever too old to begin.

May you and your family grow, hand-in-hand, together in love, faith, joy, and wisdom as you begin your prayer journey. May you seek and respond to God's presence in all that you do, and everywhere you go. May you work to further God's Kingdom in the works of love and mercy, justice and peace. May your family become one full of prayer and presence of the Lord. And may your household become a place where the light of Jesus shines for all to witness. *Amen.*

10 Everyday Prayer at Home

O*ur* Catholic tradition is rich with prayers that you can say with your family at home to supplement your own conversation with God. The following pages include common prayers as well as those created by my family. I also included information on how to begin a prayer journal with your family. I encourage you to use rote prayers with your family, especially with young children, as a means to help your children turn to God with frequency and regularity, and as a way to express your family's identity in relation to God.

✝ Sign of the Cross

We use the Sign of the Cross as a prayer and gesture at the beginning and end of our prayers as a reminder of Jesus' life and death, asking God to be present with us. It is used in many ways as a blessing: when we put the sign on our children's foreheads as we first welcome them into our community in Baptism, or when the priest blesses us and says "May Almighty God bless you, in the name of the Father, Son, and Holy Spirit," or when we anoint the sick on their foreheads. Pray this with your children as a moment to orient them in prayer, to familiarize them with our Creator, Redeemer, and Sustainer, and bless them on their daily journey.

> *In the Name of the Father,*
> *and of the Son,*
> *and of the Holy Spirit. Amen.*

My children's catechesis leader taught my children (and me!) the following prayer to say, when making the Sign of the Cross, that she learned in her training for the Catechesis of the Good Shepherd. It helped the young children in our atrium learn the proper hand motions for the Sign of the Cross:

> *For the God on my mind,*
> *The Son who is in my heart,*
> *The Holy that I reach for,*
> *And the Spirit who is near.*

Before the Gospel, we respond with "Glory to you, O Lord," and cross our foreheads, lips, and heart so that we might welcome the Word of God into our minds, lips, and hearts. Here is a prayer we can say throughout our days, so that we might know, proclaim, and love our God always:

> *Jesus,*
> *Be on my mind,*
> *On my lips,*
> *And in my heart.*

✢ Amen

We encourage our children to say "Amen" after prayers to affirm our prayer, to joyfully proclaim: So be it! We agree! We believe! There are many "Amen" songs we can sing with our children, but the following is familiar to many, as is the doxology where we sing the Great Amen in Mass.

> *Yes, we believe,*
> *We agree it is so!*
> *Amen, Amen, Let the world hear our prayer!*
> *Yes, we believe,*
> *We agree it is so!*
> *Amen, Amen, Amen.*

✢ Glory Be

> *Glory be to the Father,*
> *and to the Son,*
> *and to the Holy Spirit,*
> *as it was in the beginning,*
> *is now, and ever shall be*
> *world without end.*
> *Amen.*

✝ The Lord's Prayer

Our Father, who art in heaven,
hallowed be thy name;
thy kingdom come,
thy will be done
on earth as it is in heaven.
Give us this day our daily bread,
and forgive us our trespasses,
as we forgive others who trespass against us;
and lead us not into temptation,
but deliver us from evil.
For the kingdom,
the power and the glory are yours,
now and forever.
Amen.

✤ Blessing Your Children

Bless your children in the morning, or before bed, and mark them with a simple cross or place your hands over each body part as you pray over them. Use these or similar words.

May God
bless your forehead,
so that you can think wisely.
May God
bless your eyes,
so you can see God's presence in the world.
May God
bless your ears,
so that you can hear God's Word.
May God
bless your lips,
so that you can speak with kindness.
May God
bless your hands,
so you might do God's work.
May God
bless your bless your feet
so you may walk with Christ.
And finally, may God
bless your heart,
so that you love as God loves.

✝ Prayers in the Morning

Be with us Jesus as we wake.
Lead us through our day.
Be with us where we are,
Help us follow your way.

• • •

God, as I start my day,
I turn to you to pray.
Be with me in all I do,
help me stay close to you.

• • •

Good morning, dear Jesus,
this day is for you.
Please be with me,
in all I think, say, and do.

• • •

✝ Blessings before Meals

The following, from my church community's First Communion preparation, is sung to the tune of "Edelweiss." My kids loved singing this before meals.

Thanks to God,
praise and thanks!
Lord, we gather together.

From the earth
you have brought
bread we break now together.
All who hungered
shall bless your name,
bless your name forever.
Thanks to God,
praise and thanks!
Lord, you bring us together.

• • •

Bless us, O Lord,
and these, thy gifts,
which we are about to receive
from thy bounty.
Through Christ, our Lord.
Amen.

• • •

God is great,
God is good!
Let us thank him
for our food.
By his hands
we all are fed.
Give us, Lord,
our daily bread.

• • •

✟ Prayers before Bed

Now I lay me down to sleep,
I pray the Lord my soul to keep.
God's love be with me through the night,
And wake me with the morning light.

• • •

Goodnight, dear Lord,
to you I say:
thank you for
this beautiful day!

✟ Everyday Prayers

Help me, God
to do what's right
for this I pray
with all my might.

• • •

You are so good to me Jesus,
I thank you each day
for giving me all I need,
and loving me in every way.

• • •

✝ Five Finger Prayer

Another simple way to remind your children to pray is to use their fingers. The Five Finger Prayer has been around for a while, and has been attributed to Pope Francis while he was still Archbishop in Argentina. The basics are as follows, although you can use whatever works for your family. This can be particularly helpful for younger children (and even adults!) as using your fingers is a simple, visual reminder that can help your child to pray.

THUMB *Pray to those who are close to you: your parents, your siblings, your immediate friends and family.*

POINTER FINGER *Pray for those who point you in the right direction: your teachers and catechists.*

MIDDLE FINGER *Your tallest finger reminds you to pray for leaders, in your local communities, government, and church leaders.*

RING FINGER *Your weakest finger reminds you to pray for the needs of others: those who are hurting, those who are sad, anyone in need.*

PINKY FINGER *Your smallest finger reminds you to pray for your own needs.*

✝ Prayer Journal

Another activity to do with your family that can really go hand in hand with and enrich your prayer life, is to create a prayer journal. It allows for a hands-on approach to prayer that many children who are tactile, kinesthetic, or visual learners, really thrive at. It also allows for a bit of creativity for those who like to write or draw to bring their gifts to the family prayer. These journals can be made separately by each individual in the house, or the family can create one for the entire family to contribute. Prayer journals are a way to visibly make prayer a habitual act, with the hopes that seeing their prayers in writing will help them recognize and visualize God's presence in their daily lives.

These journals can be individualized, but the general idea is that you create a journal (there are specific notebooks available at Christian stores or online, but any notebook would do nicely) and fill it with prayers and drawings daily that remind you of God's presence. Here are some suggestions:

- Have your children write down (or you can write them down if they are too young) or draw their prayers, whether they are prayers of praise, thanksgiving, blessings, intercessions, or petitions.

- Have your children share their prayers with you; create a conversation about God.

- Write down Bible verses or maxims that your children are thinking about or that you are reading as a family. Encourage them to read these verses periodically throughout the day or week to contemplate their meaning.

- Have children draw something that helps them think about God. It could be church, your garden, or the gifts you receive from God. Let your children be creative!

- Share your joys with God.

- Write about what God has done for you today and how God has acted in your life.

- How does God make you feel?

- Remember prayers of thanksgiving. Get in a habit of thanking God!

- Encourage your children to think about how God answered your prayers of petitions and inter-cessions, and write that down.

- Try to set aside a regular time for your children to write and draw in their journal. This gives them a daily reminder of God's presence in their lives!

- Share the prayer journal with other family members to encourage each other to see and think about God in new ways.

✟ A Model for Family Prayer at Home

- Gather in a Prayerful Silence
- Share Prayers of Gratitude

> *Thank you God for the people in our lives.*
> *Thank you God for being with us.*
> *Thank you God for your many gifts.*
> *Thank you God for our spiritual gifts.*

✟ Intercessions

> *Response to each: Lord, hear our prayer.*
> *Pray for our individual needs.*
> *Pray for the needs of our family and friends.*
> *Pray for the needs of our church.*
> *Pray for the needs of our larger community.*
> *Pray for the needs of our world.*
> *Pray for peace and justice, the needs of the poor*
> *and vulnerable, human rights,*
> *dignity for all, and care for our earth.*
> *Pray in silence for the prayers still in our hearts.*

✟ Reflection and Conversation

- Talk about God with your children.
- Try to understand God more.

✟ Include Other Forms of Prayer

- Sing a song.
- Read a Bible verse and pray together.

Additional Resources

The following resources may help you on your journey in growing a family prayer life.

- *Celebrating Sunday for Catholic Families*. Published yearly. Chicago: Liturgy Training Publications.

- *Catholic Household Blessings and Prayers*. United States Conference of Catholic Bishops.

- Jeep, Elizabeth McMahon. *Blessings and Prayers through the Year: A Resource for School and Parish*. Chicago: Liturgy Training Publications, 1994.

- Nussbaum, Melissa Musick. *My First Holy Communion: Sunday Mass and Daily Prayers*. Revised edition. Chicago: Liturgy Training Publications, 2011.

About the Author

Karla Hardersen is a wife and mother of three teenagers. She has studied religion and theology at the undergraduate and graduate levels and was a Bernardin Scholar at the Catholic Theological Union, Chicago. She is an active member of a Catholic faith community, where she has also been an assistant catechist for the Catechesis of the Good Shepherd program.